Original title:
Lessons in Trust

Copyright © 2024 Swan Charm
All rights reserved.

Author: Sabrina Sarvik
ISBN HARDBACK: 978-9916-89-769-0
ISBN PAPERBACK: 978-9916-89-770-6
ISBN EBOOK: 978-9916-89-771-3

## The Wisdom of Promises

In the quiet dawn, where shadows play,
The whispers of hope guide the way.
With hearts attuned to a sacred call,
We gather in love, together we stand tall.

Each promise spoken, a binding thread,
In the tapestry of faith, where fears are shed.
With hands uplifted, we search for the light,
For in each vow, shines the strength to fight.

In valleys low or mountains high,
The spirit of trust lifts us to the sky.
For every tear that falls from grace,
Is a lesson learned in this blessed place.

Through trials faced and burdens borne,
The wisdom of promises, like roses, has grown.
In silence we ponder, in prayer we find,
The power of love, divinely aligned.

So let us embrace the solemn decree,
In unity held, our souls set free.
With each word cherished, in hearts profound,
The wisdom of promises in grace is found.

## **Tides of Fidelity**

In the quiet dawn, faith takes its stand,
Each wave a promise, shaped by His hand.
Through storms we gather, our hearts intertwined,
In the sea of His love, our souls are aligned.

With each ebb and flow, our spirits renew,
In whispers of trust, His words ring true.
We walk on the shore, where grace softly calls,
Guided by the light, that never falls.

## Wings of Devotion

On the breeze of prayer, our hearts take flight,
Soaring above, in the warm morning light.
With each fluttering beat, we rise and we sing,
In the sanctuary's hush, our praises take wing.

Through valleys of doubt, our spirits ascend,
In the arms of His mercy, our hearts mend.
With wings of devotion, we follow the way,
In the promise of love, we find our stay.

## The Mirror of Integrity

In the reflection of truth, there lies our grace,
A faithful heart, in its rightful place.
With every choice made, we honor His call,
In the mirror of integrity, we stand tall.

Each action a word, in the silence we speak,
A path illuminated, though often unique.
In the light of His gaze, our souls unite,
With courage and honor, we walk in His light.

## Oracles of the Heart

In the stillness of night, wisdom softly stirs,
The oracles of the heart, in whispers, concur.
Through trials and triumphs, we listen and learn,
In the quiet of faith, our spirits will burn.

With each tender moment, the truth shall resound,
In the echoes of love, our purpose is found.
In the tapestry woven with threads of His grace,
The oracles guide us, through time and through space.

## Chronicles of the Heart

In silence, whispers of truth reside,
A tapestry woven, our souls abide.
With every heartbeat, faith's gentle call,
Guides us through trials, lest we fall.

In shadows cast, where doubt may loom,
The light within will always bloom.
With each step taken on this sacred way,
Hope ignites the dawn of each new day.

From ashes rise, the spirit soars high,
With love as the anchor, we touch the sky.
In unity binding, we find our art,
The everlasting chronicles of the heart.

## **The Union of Spirits**

Two souls entwined, a dance divine,
In sacred union, hearts align.
With vows unspoken echoing clear,
Our spirits merge, casting out fear.

In the quiet moments, faith takes flight,
Hand in hand, we embrace the light.
As rivers meet in expansive grace,
Together we journey, in love's embrace.

Through trials faced, our bond grows strong,
In sacred harmony, we belong.
With each breath taken, our spirits share,
The union forged in love and prayer.

## The Melody of Commitment

A symphony played with heartstrings true,
In every note, I promise to you.
Through storms and trials, we shall compose,
The melody of love, where devotion flows.

In rhythms of laughter, and tears we find,
The sacred harmony, forever entwined.
With each chorus sung, our spirits rise,
For in commitment lies love's sweet ties.

Let the world hear our song, vibrant and bold,
A testament to the stories of old.
In the dance of eternity, we'll forever play,
The melody of commitment, come what may.

## The Divine Assurance

In the quiet dusk, a promise unfolds,
The Divine whispers truths that it holds.
Through every trial, we are never alone,
With love as our guide, we find our home.

In moments of doubt, when shadows creep,
The light of the heavens bids us to leap.
With faith as our armor, we step forth bold,
In the warmth of assurance, our hearts behold.

Each blessing bestowed, a gentle embrace,
Reminding our spirits of grace in this place.
In the tapestry woven by hands from above,
We find strength and solace, in Divine Love.

## The Lighthouse of Devotion

In twilight's glow, we seek the light,
A beacon shining through the night.
With hearts ablaze, we forge ahead,
In faith and love, our souls are fed.

Each prayer a wave, crashing at sea,
Guiding our paths, setting us free.
Together strong, we rise and stand,
In the warmth of His gentle hand.

When storms arise and shadows fall,
We find our strength, we heed the call.
For in His grace, we find our peace,
Our lighthouse stands, our fears release.

So let us gather, share the flame,
In unity, we praise His name.
With every step, our spirits soar,
In the lighthouse, forevermore.

## **Roses of Rely**

In gardens lush where roses bloom,
Our faith takes root dispelling gloom.
Each petal soft, a prayer unfolds,
A story of love in hues of gold.

Through trials faced, we stand as one,
In joy and sorrow, love is spun.
A fragrant breath, we lift our voice,
In trust we find, we still rejoice.

Rely on Him, our hearts entwined,
With gratitude, our souls aligned.
For every thorn, a lesson learned,
Through every trial, His love returned.

In every bloom, a promise speaks,
As faith abounds, so love increases.
We gather roses, side by side,
In the garden, our hearts abide.

## The Fortress of Assurance

In the shadows, we find our place,
A fortress built on love and grace.
With walls of hope, we stand secure,
In every trial, we shall endure.

When doubts arise and fears take flight,
We seek the truth, embrace the light.
With every prayer, our spirits rise,
In the fortress strong, our faith defies.

Each moment shared, our hearts entwined,
In love's embrace, we are defined.
Together here, we bear the fight,
In the fortress, we find our might.

No storm can break this sacred space,
Our souls united in deep embrace.
In trust we dwell, in peace we dwell,
In the fortress of assurance, all is well.

## **Seasons of Trust**

In spring's embrace, new life is born,
With whispered promises each dawn.
As flowers bloom and rivers flow,
We find the light, our spirits grow.

In summer's warmth, we share our dreams,
In trusting hearts, love gently gleams.
Through laughter shared and moments bright,
We walk together in the light.

As autumn whispers, leaves will fall,
We gather close, we heed the call.
In seasons change, our hearts remain,
In trust, we find joy amidst pain.

When winter's chill draws near, we stand,
Together held by faith's warm hand.
Through every season, we will find,
In trust we thrive, our hearts aligned.

## Sacred Bonds

In holy silence, we unite,
Bonds of spirit, pure and bright.
In faith we gather, hand in hand,
Together walking, a sacred land.

Whispers echo through the night,
Guiding hearts with gentle light.
Each prayer a thread, woven tight,
In love's embrace, we find our might.

With humble hearts, we seek the truth,
In every moment, in every youth.
A tapestry of grace and care,
In kindness shared, our souls laid bare.

Through trials faced, we grow anew,
Stronger in faith, our love rings true.
With every step, a promise made,
In unity, our fears allayed.

Let spirits soar, break every chain,
In joyful worship, we find refrain.
Together we rise, with hope imbued,
In sacred bonds, our lives renewed.

# Echoes of Confidence

In the stillness, a voice does call,
Awakening courage, igniting all.
Whispers of hope, like a gentle breeze,
Fill our hearts, bringing us ease.

With every sunrise, new strength bestowed,
On paths of trust, our spirits flowed.
In echoes of confidence, we stand tall,
Together we rise, never to fall.

A light within, that never dims,
In unity's warmth, our faith begins.
In shadows that fall, our purpose clear,
With every heartbeat, banish fear.

Through trials faced, our souls aligned,
In love's embrace, our spirits entwined.
With steadfast hearts, we boldly stride,
In echoes of confidence, we abide.

Each step we take, in grace we sow,
In trust we flourish, in love we grow.
Together we chant, in chorus we sing,
In joyful harmony, our spirits take wing.

## The Covenant of Hearts

In the quiet, our promises lay,
Hearts entwined in a sacred way.
Through joy and sorrow, we stand as one,
In the covenant of hearts, life's journey begun.

With every heartbeat, the vows we keep,
In solace found, our love runs deep.
Together we weather the storms that rage,
In faith's embrace, we turn the page.

A tapestry woven with threads of grace,
Each moment cherished, no time to waste.
In laughter shared, in tears that flow,
In the covenant of hearts, our spirits grow.

Through trials faced, we lift our voice,
In unity strong, we rejoice.
With every dawn, our path is clear,
In love's embrace, we cast out fear.

Together we journey, hand in hand,
In sacred trust, forever we stand.
In the covenant of hearts, we find our peace,
In love's sweet bond, may our burdens cease.

## **Pilgrimage of Promise**

On this journey, our spirits rise,
With every step, we seek the skies.
In the pilgrimage of promise, we tread,
Following signs where angels led.

Through valleys low and mountains high,
In faith we wander, no need to sigh.
With hearts ablaze, we carry the flame,
In every encounter, we share His name.

Each road we travel, a lesson learned,
In humble gratitude, our hearts are turned.
As stars align, our pathways blend,
On sacred journeys, our love extends.

Together we walk, through fire and rain,
In trials faced, our strength we gain.
With every breath, we honor the call,
In the pilgrimage of promise, we stand tall.

Let whispers of hope guide our way,
In faith and courage, we choose to stay.
In the light of grace, let our spirits shine,
On this pilgrimage of promise, forever divine.

## The Harmony of Assurance

In the stillness of dawn, we rise,
With faith unfurled, we seek the skies.
In gentle whispers, hope is found,
In sacred light, our hearts are bound.

When shadows fall, and doubts converge,
Through prayer and love, we find our surge.
In tranquil waters, peace will reign,
In every loss, there is gain.

With each soft breath, we share this grace,
In every challenge, we find our place.
Together in trust, we walk the way,
In every night, there comes a day.

For in each soul, a spark ignites,
A journey guided by holy lights.
In unity strong, we face the storm,
With hearts aligned, we are reborn.

In the warmth of love, we stand as one,
In the light of faith, our battles won.
With harmony's song, we rise above,
In assurance found, we dwell in love.

## Mosaic of Dependability

In every piece, a story we weave,
Through trials faced, we learn to believe.
Each fragment shines with its own hue,
In the grand design, our hearts are true.

With open hands, we share our toil,
In service given, our spirits uncoil.
Together we build, with hope in sight,
In every moment, we choose the light.

In the tapestry of life, we stand,
With threads of kindness, a steady hand.
Each voice united in sacred song,
In loyalty found, we all belong.

When storms arise, we hold our ground,
In trust and faith, our strength is found.
With every heartbeat, we call to pray,
In dependability, we find our way.

In the love of kin, through joy and strife,
In bonds unbroken, we celebrate life.
With every smile, a promise to keep,
In this mosaic, our souls are deep.

# The Language of the Heart

In silence spoken, the heart's refrain,
A gentle whisper through joy and pain.
With every beat, love's rhythm flows,
In every glance, the spirit knows.

Through kindness poured, we find our speech,
In open arms, we seek to reach.
Each act of grace, a language clear,
In unity's dance, we draw near.

When words may fail, and silence reigns,
Through heartfelt gestures, love remains.
In shared compassion, our voices rise,
In tenderness found, there are no lies.

With each embrace, the truth unfolds,
In warmth and light, a story told.
Through laughter shared, and tears we shed,
In the language of the heart, we're led.

In every moment, we seek to learn,
Through patience offered, our souls discern.
With love as our guide, we walk anew,
In the language of the heart, we find our view.

## Reverence in Union

In quiet spaces, we gather as one,
With reverent hearts, a journey begun.
In every prayer, a calling clear,
In sacred union, we hold dear.

With lifted hands, we share the grace,
In every heartbeat, we find a place.
Through sacred rhythms, our spirits soar,
In harmony's embrace, we yearn for more.

When tempests rage, and shadows fall,
In unity's strength, we rise and call.
With open hearts, we light the way,
In reverence found, we choose to stay.

With every bond, a covenant made,
In trust and hope, our fears cascade.
In love's reflection, we find our truth,
In reverence shared, we nurture our youth.

As one we stand, in faith embraced,
In every moment, our hearts are traced.
Through unity's song, we journey far,
In reverence in union, we are who we are.

# Chambers of Loyalty

In chambers deep where spirits dwell,
A steadfast heart resounds the bell.
With whispers soft, the truth we find,
In bonds unbroken, souls entwined.

Through trials faced, we stand as one,
Beneath the gaze of warming sun.
With every step, our minds align,
In loyalty, our souls do shine.

When shadows fall, we rise anew,
With faith as guide, we journey through.
Each promise made, a sacred thread,
Together bound, where love is spread.

Let hearts be strong, let voices sing,
In unity, we'll spread our wings.
In chambers sacred, we declare,
Our loyalty, a fervent prayer.

## The Flame of Belief

A flicker glows within the night,
A flame of hope, a beacon bright.
Through storms that rage and winds that howl,
In darkest times, we raise a prowl.

This flame ignites the hearts of men,
With fervent zeal, we rise again.
In every doubt, it brightly burns,
A lesson learned as spirit turns.

With hands outstretched, we share the light,
In every heart, it takes its flight.
Together bound, we'll never fail,
In unity, our dreams set sail.

Oh, sacred fire, our guiding star,
No distance great can keep us far.
For in belief, we find our way,
A vibrant path, come what may.

## Whispers from the Divine

In quiet moments, whispers flow,
A sacred voice, the heart must know.
Through every trial, hear it near,
In gentle tones, it calms our fear.

The winds carry a soft refrain,
Of love that mends all forms of pain.
Each word bestowed, a cherished gift,
To spirits lost, hope gives a lift.

When silence reigns and shadows creep,
The whispers call, the soul to keep.
With tender grace, they guide the way,
In faith's embrace, we choose to stay.

Let every whisper shape our fate,
In the divine, we congregate.
Through listening hearts, let peace abide,
In whispered truths, let faith reside.

## The Legacy of Faith

A legacy built on ancient ground,
In every heart, traditions found.
Through generations, wisdom soars,
In every lesson, hope restores.

With steady hands, we pass the flame,
In silent prayers, we speak its name.
From past to present, threads we weave,
In faith's embrace, we dare believe.

Let stories shared resound like bells,
In every tale, the spirit swells.
From mother's voice to child's sweet ear,
In whispered dreams, the path is clear.

Through trials faced and glory won,
The legacy flows, we are all one.
In faith we stand, through storms we tread,
With hearts united, the light is spread.

## Resilience in Reverence

In the shadows, faith does rise,
A beacon bright in troubled skies.
With every trial, a strength we gain,
In sacred whispers, love remains.

Each storm will pass, as dust we tread,
On sacred ground where angels led.
When hearts are weary, hope shall bloom,
In reverence, we find our room.

Through valleys deep, we walk with grace,
In prayerful moments, we find our place.
With every tear, a lesson learned,
For every flicker, a fire burned.

Guided by light, the path unfolds,
In sacred texts, the truth is told.
Resilience woven through each thread,
In reverence, we forge ahead.

## **Stones of Certainty**

Upon the rock, our hopes do dwell,
A fortress strong, where spirits swell.
Each stone a promise, steadfast, sure,
In life's embrace, we shall endure.

With hands uplifted, we find our strength,
In every challenge, we go the length.
Through trials fierce, our faith a guide,
In unity, we will abide.

The weight of doubt may cloud our view,
Yet stones of certainty shine through.
With every heartbeat, we proclaim,
In steadfast love, we rise again.

Bound by a vision, hearts entwined,
In sacred silence, truth we find.
Each stone a testament to grace,
In faith's embrace, we find our place.

## The Savior's Embrace

In quiet moments, voices call,
A gentle touch, the Savior's thrall.
With arms stretched wide, He welcomes all,
In love, we rise, not once we fall.

Through burdens heavy, hope will soar,
In the embrace, we are restored.
With every whisper, fears subside,
In truth and light, we shall abide.

Together we journey, side by side,
With faith our compass, love our guide.
The Savior's heart, a refuge deep,
In holy peace, our souls shall leap.

In every heartache, grace will flow,
With love abundant, we shall grow.
The Savior's promise, clear and bright,
In His embrace, we find the light.

## **Illuminations of the Heart**

In stillness found, the heart ignites,
Illuminations spark the nights.
With love as fire, hope will blaze,
In sacred moments, we give praise.

Through trials faced, our spirits rise,
In depth of sorrow, wisdom lies.
With open hearts, we seek the light,
In unity, all wrongs made right.

The path may twist, with shadows cast,
Yet in the dark, our faith holds fast.
With every heartbeat, joy will sing,
Illuminations, our offering.

Through every sorrow, love reveals,
In gentle touch, the heart appeals.
With eyes wide open, we shall see,
In love's embrace, we all are free.

## Anchors of Conviction

In the storm, faith stands true,
Holding fast, we are renewed.
With each prayer, our spirits soar,
Anchored deep to Heaven's shore.

Guiding light through darkest night,
In His grace, we find our might.
Whispers of love, gentle and clear,
In His embrace, we have no fear.

Roots that stretch through trials wide,
In unity, we shall abide.
Through the tempest, our hearts stay strong,
Together, we rise where we belong.

Promises etched in sacred stone,
In our hearts, His love is known.
With each heartbeat, a sacred vow,
Anchors of conviction show us how.

Through every doubt and every tear,
His presence calms all our fears.
In the silence, His voice we find,
Guiding us with a steadfast mind.

## The Veil of Reassurance

Wrapped in grace, we find our peace,
Under His love, our worries cease.
With every breath, a quiet hymn,
The veil of reassurance, soft and dim.

In shadows cast by doubt and pain,
His light shines through, breaks every chain.
In the garden, whispers of sighs,
Petals fall where hope never dies.

Each gentle touch, a promise made,
In His arms, all fears shall fade.
With every trial, we learn to trust,
The veil of reassurance, a sacred must.

Through veils of doubt and wandering nights,
His truth emerges, guiding lights.
In fellowship, we gather near,
Wrapped in love, we cast away fear.

In silent prayers, we find our home,
With Him beside us, we shall roam.
Through every path and unknown shore,
The veil of reassurance, forevermore.

## Guiding Stars

In the heavens, bright and clear,
Guiding stars that draw us near.
With each twinkle, a sign of grace,
Leading us to the sacred place.

Through trials faced and valleys low,
His stars above, a steadfast glow.
In the night, they shine so bright,
Gifts of hope in darkest night.

With every prayer, we chase the light,
Finding strength in His pure sight.
In their glow, our spirits rise,
Guiding stars across the skies.

In unity, we walk the path,
Two hearts bound in hope's sweet bath.
With each heartbeat, we soar afar,
Navigating by the guiding star.

Together, we embrace the dawn,
With His promise, fear is gone.
Through every storm, our spirits lay,
Guided by stars, we find our way.

## The Heart's Testament

In silence deep, the heart does speak,
Testament of love, pure and meek.
Each beat a promise, each sigh a prayer,
In faith's embrace, we lay it bare.

Through whispered vows and gentle grace,
In every trial, He finds a place.
With every joy and every tear,
The heart's testament, always near.

In unity, we rise as one,
With love's light shining like the sun.
Through every wound and every scar,
The heart's testament, our guiding star.

In sacred moments, we stand tall,
Together we rise, divided we fall.
With gratitude, we lift our voice,
In the heart's testament, we rejoice.

Through every shadow, through every dawn,
Faithful and true, we carry on.
With love as our shield, fierce and bright,
The heart's testament shines in the night.

## The Quietude of Faith

In stillness, hearts do seek,
The whispers of the Divine.
In shadows, light will speak,
Guiding hands, oh so benign.

In prayer, the soul finds rest,
With each breath, a sacred grace.
In trials, we are blessed,
With love that time can't erase.

Through storms, our spirits soar,
On wings of hope, we rise.
In silence, we implore,
Eternal truths, the skies.

In the depth of night, we call,
A beacon in the dark.
With faith, we stand tall,
For our hearts hold the spark.

In the quietude of prayer,
We find strength for the plight.
In His presence, despair
Melts away into light.

## The Loom of Commitment

Threads of purpose intertwine,
In the fabric of our hearts.
Each promise a sacred line,
Crafting wholeness through the arts.

In service, we weave our ties,
With love that never frays.
A tapestry that defies,
The doubts of earthly ways.

With every stitch, we align,
Heaven's intent, our creed.
In unity, we divine,
The grace in every deed.

Commitment, a sacred thread,
Bound by trust, not by fear.
In every word we spread,
Faith's banner flying near.

In this loom, we stand as one,
Working with hands and heart.
In His light, a mission spun,
In love, we find our part.

## Cascades of Grace

From mountains high, the waters flow,
A gift from heavens up above.
In each drop, the blessings glow,
A testament of endless love.

Through valleys deep, His mercy streams,
Refreshing every parched terrain.
In our weakness, hope redeems,
With every loss, we gain.

The rivers sing in harmony,
A chorus of the angels' voice.
In the currents, we are free,
In grace, we rejoice.

In flowing waves, His truth prevails,
No burden too great to bear.
With faith, we ride the trails,
Abounding in His care.

Cascades of grace, forever near,
In every heart, a sacred space.
With open arms, we draw Him near,
In love's embrace, we find our place.

## Archangels of Loyalty

In shadows cast by earthly strife,
The archangels guard our way.
With loyalty, they bring life,
In their wings, we find our stay.

With fiery swords and gentle might,
They watch o'er every soul's plight.
In their presence, all is right,
Guiding us toward the light.

Through trials, they steadfast stand,
A promise of the Lord so true.
In their embrace, we understand,
Loyalty in all we do.

In harmony, they sing our praise,
Elevating hearts in prayer.
In our journey, they amaze,
With grace beyond compare.

Archangels, fierce in love's decree,
With loyalty, our hearts entwine.
In our lives, let it be,
A testament, His design.

## Sculptures of Faith

In silence, the marble waits,
Chiseled by divine hands.
Each fracture tells a story,
Of hope that understands.

With every stroke of grace,
Form rises from the stone.
Faith, a quiet echo,
In the heart, it finds home.

Through storms, the artists toil,
In patience, light breaks through.
Sculptures stand in glory,
Reflecting love so true.

In the gallery of dreams,
Each figure speaks aloud.
With spirits intertwined,
We stand amongst the crowd.

Chiseled in the shadow,
A testament to time.
In every crack and flaw,
Beauty's voice, sublime.

## Threads of Kinship

In the tapestry of life,
Connections softly weave.
Threads of love and laughter,
In hearts, we must believe.

Across rivers and mountains,
Each bond holds strong and tight.
United in our journey,
We gather in the light.

As seasons change their colors,
In warmth, we find our way.
The fabric of our spirits,
Strengthens day by day.

Through trials, we discover,
What truly brings us near.
The threads that tie us deeply,
Whisper love, not fear.

In the quilt of our stories,
Relatives near and far.
Together we are brighter,
Guided by a star.

## The Compass of Trust

In shadows, hope ignites,
A compass leads the way.
With every faithful step,
We find the light of day.

Trust, a gentle whisper,
Beneath the cloak of night.
It navigates our souls,
Drawing paths of clear sight.

When storms of doubt surround,
The heart's direction stays.
Each moment filled with faith,
Carries us through the maze.

The needle points to grace,
In love's familiar face.
We travel onward bravely,
In trust, we find our place.

With every choice we make,
We plant a seed of truth.
The compass never falters,
Guiding our hidden roots.

### The Wisdom of Vulnerability

In the garden of our hearts,
Soft petals start to bloom.
Vulnerability speaks,
In moments full of room.

Each tear that falls is strength,
A truth that sets us free.
In openness, we blossom,
In love, we learn to see.

There's power in surrender,
In sharing all our scars.
For in the cracks of courage,
Our light can shine like stars.

Embracing what is real,
Invites the world to stay.
Together, hand in hand,
We journey on the way.

Through tender acts of grace,
We cultivate our trust.
In wisdom, we find solace,
In love, we rise from dust.

## Threads of the Divine

In the silence, whispers flow,
Threads of grace, in hearts they sow.
Bound by faith, we rise and pray,
Guided gently, the light of day.

Every soul, a sacred thread,
Woven tight, where love is spread.
In the tapestry we find,
Unity in every kind.

Through trials, strength is gained,
In the storm, His love remained.
With each stitch, a battle won,
Life's a journey, never done.

Oft we stumble, yet we stand,
Held by grace, a guiding hand.
In the fabric of the night,
Threads unite, the heart takes flight.

## Waters of Understanding

In the depths, where spirits flow,
Wisdom's tide will gently glow.
Water's grace, it quenches thirst,
In every soul, compassion burst.

From the river, lessons glean,
Gentle currents, serene and clean.
As we drink, the heart expands,
In the stillness, love commands.

Every wave brings tides of peace,
In the waters, sorrows cease.
Flowing gently, hold me near,
In this realm, I feel no fear.

I am one with all that's pure,
In the depths, my soul is sure.
From the wellspring, life unfolds,
In every drop, the truth it holds.

## **The Bond Beyond Sight**

In unseen realms, we intertwine,
A bond so deep, a love divine.
Hearts aligned, though far apart,
In the silence, we find our heart.

Beyond the veil, our spirits soar,
Together strong, forevermore.
In every breath, a whispered thread,
Love's embrace, where angels tread.

Though the world may fade away,
In the dark, we find our way.
Hand in hand, though not in sight,
Faith will guide us through the night.

Every spirit, a sacred flame,
Burning bright, in His great name.
In the stillness, hearts will sing,
Beyond the veil, our praises ring.

## Starlight in the Dark

When shadows fall, the night takes form,
Starlight glows, a gentle warm.
Guiding souls through paths unknown,
In the dark, we're never alone.

Each twinkle holds a hope profound,
In the silence, love is found.
Celestial whispers fill the night,
Leading hearts towards the light.

With every star, a story told,
Of faith enduring, brave and bold.
In the cosmos, we'll unite,
As stardust dances, pure delight.

Trust the journey, walk the way,
In the dark, let faith hold sway.
For even when the night is long,
Starlight shines, we'll find our song.

## The Stone of Certainty

In faith we stand, a steadfast stone,
With prayers whispered, never alone.
Our hearts united, a sacred bond,
In His embrace, we grow more fond.

In trials faced, our courage shines,
Through darkest nights, His word aligns.
A beacon bright, His love our guide,
With every step, in Him, we bide.

The path is rough, yet we shall stay,
With every breath, we choose to pray.
Our doubts transformed, like dust to gold,
In this covenant, we are bold.

Each stone we lay, a promise made,
In trust, our fears begin to fade.
Together here, we build our life,
With hope and grace, amidst the strife.

For in our hearts, certainty sings,
With faith as strong, on such truth clings.
Our souls entwined, like vines do soar,
In Him, our peace forevermore.

## **Pledges in Prayer**

With hands held high, we call your name,
In whispered prayers, our hearts aflame.
Each pledge we make, in love we stand,
United, we seek Your guiding hand.

Oh, Lord, we vow to serve in light,
To spread Your love, to shine so bright.
In every soul, may kindness flow,
Through acts of grace, together grow.

We gather close, as family dear,
In times of joy, in times of fear.
Our hopes entwined, like roots so strong,
In faith's embrace, we sing our song.

With every breath, our spirits soar,
Pledges spoken, forevermore.
In silence shared, we find our way,
In prayerful trust, we rise each day.

As sun does rise and stars do gleam,
Our hearts reflect a sacred dream.
In unity, we walk this path,
With love abiding, we find our math.

## Blessings of Openness

In gentle hearts, we seek to know,
The whispered truths that softly flow.
With arms wide open, we embrace,
Each soul we meet, a sacred space.

Through every tear, a lesson learned,
In love's embrace, our spirits turned.
With honesty, we share our plight,
Together stepping into light.

In vulnerability, true strength lies,
We share our fears, our hopes arise.
An open heart, a vibrant song,
In diversity, we all belong.

With kindness shared, our burdens fade,
In every moment, love displayed.
Each blessing found in giving grace,
In openness, we find our place.

So let the walls around us fall,
In His embrace, we hear the call.
With hands outstretched, we offer prayer,
In blessings shared, our love laid bare.

## The Light of Trustworthiness

In shadows deep, His light will shine,
Creating paths, both bright and fine.
With trusted hearts, we journey forth,
In every step, we find our worth.

A promise held, through thick and thin,
In every loss, in every win.
With faithful eyes, we seek the truth,
In every moment, reclaim youth.

In trials faced, we stand as one,
In trust regained, our battles won.
Through honesty, our spirits meet,
In faithful deeds, our hearts repeat.

This sacred bond, a treasure true,
In every word, our faith renew.
With gentle grace, we learn to see,
The light of trust, forever free.

So let us walk with heads held high,
In His embrace, we need not shy.
For in each heart, His message spreads,
In trustworthiness, our spirit treads.

## The Altar of Truth

Upon the altar, faith we lay,
Whispers of love, lighting the way.
In silence we gather, hearts entwined,
Seeking the solace, the spirit aligned.

Rays of wisdom flicker bright,
Guiding the lost in the night.
Truth like a river flows on,
In every heart, a sacred song.

Pillars of hope rise high above,
Bound in the silence of pure love.
With each supplication, we trust,
In the embrace of faith, we must.

Voices meld in a sacred chime,
Echoing love through space and time.
Together we stand, hand in hand,
A circle of light in this holy land.

In the stillness, our spirits soar,
To the altar of truth, we seek more.
Where shadows fade, and light holds sway,
In the arms of grace, we shall stay.

## **Radiance of Loyalty**

In the glow of devotion, hearts ignite,
Beneath the stars, our spirits unite.
With every promise, we stand tall,
In loyalty's embrace, we won't fall.

Hands clasped in prayer, we seek the way,
Through trials faced, come what may.
In shadows dim, our fire burns,
With every lesson, our spirit learns.

Journeying forth, side by side,
In truth and faith, we shall abide.
The radiance of loyalty shines true,
Reflecting grace in all we do.

With every whisper, love's refrain,
In storms of life, through joy and pain.
Together we thrive, hearts so bright,
In the dance of devotion, pure light.

Here in the bond, our souls reside,
In loyalty's name, we take pride.
Through every passage, we shall steer,
Radiating love, year after year.

## Windows to the Promise

Through windows of hope, the light streams in,
Casting shadows where doubt has been.
With open hearts, we dare to see,
The promise of tomorrow, wild and free.

Each dawn unveils a canvas rare,
Brushing our souls with gentle care.
In the colors of faith, we find our way,
Drawing strength from the light of day.

With eyes alight, we dream anew,
In every challenge, courage grew.
Windows ajar, we breathe the grace,
Embracing the journey, time's sweet face.

Voices adorned with promises bright,
Together we stand, ready for flight.
In faith's embrace, our spirits soar,
In unity gathered, we seek for more.

In the tapestry woven by trust,
With every thread, we rise, we must.
Windows to the promise, open wide,
A sanctuary where love can abide.

## The Emissary of Goodwill

In every act of kindness shown,
The emissary of goodwill is known.
With gentle hearts and open hands,
We weave the fabric of love's demands.

Through every smile and soft embrace,
We light the world, a sacred place.
In every moment, we find our way,
Guided by compassion, day by day.

With footsteps sure, we walk as one,
Under the light of the rising sun.
In service given, our spirits rise,
Reflecting hope in each other's eyes.

In whispers shared, and laughter sweet,
The dance of goodwill, we repeat.
Together we stand, united and true,
As emissaries, our purpose shines through.

In the tapestry of life, we weave,
The threads of love, we shall believe.
With every heartbeat, let goodwill flow,
A gift to the world, in faith, we grow.

## The Horizon of Reassurance

Beneath the vast and azure sky,
We seek the light that draws us near.
In whispers soft, the heavens sigh,
A balm for every doubt and fear.

Each star a promise shining bright,
Guiding us through the darkest night.
For in His grace, we find our might,
Our spirits lifted, pure delight.

The dawn unveils a gentle glow,
Hope dances in the morning's hue.
Through trials, we shall learn and grow,
In faith, we find our path anew.

The horizon speaks of calm and peace,
Where burdens fade, and joy can soar.
In this embrace, our fears release,
Divine assurance, evermore.

Hand in hand, we walk the way,
With hearts aligned, our souls ignite.
In love's embrace, we choose to stay,
Together, guided by the light.

## Fount of Validity

In quietude, the truth reveals,
A fountain flows with waters pure.
It quenches thirst, the soul it heals,
In faith we find what will endure.

Each drop a blessing from above,
Sustaining all who seek its grace.
In every heartbeat, feel the love,
In silence, find the sacred space.

From depths profound, wisdom does rise,
A gentle stream that guides the way.
With open hearts, we seek the skies,
As light of truth dispels the gray.

In every question, lies the chance,
To delve into the depths of thought.
With reverent hearts, we join the dance,
To find the truths that we have sought.

So let the fount flow ever strong,
Its waters cleanse our weary souls.
In harmony, we sing our song,
In unity, the spirit rolls.

## **Echoing Amen**

In prayer we find our voices rise,
A chorus sweet, a sacred bond.
Each word a spark beneath the skies,
In faith, together we respond.

Amen, we echo, hearts aligned,
In harmony, our spirits blend.
With every chant, the soul refined,
As love and grace in us descend.

The stillness holds what words can't say,
In silence, we begin to feel.
With open hearts, we kneel and pray,
Inviting grace to help us heal.

In gathering, the light does grow,
Each whisper shared a radiant beam.
Through every struggle, we will throw,
Our hopes and prayers, one sacred dream.

Together, bound by faith's embrace,
We lift our voices, strong and true.
In every echo, love and grace,
In every Amen, God renews.

## **The Soul's Refuge**

In shadows deep, the heart can roam,
Yet in His arms, we find our home.
Each sigh a prayer that lifts the night,
In sacred stillness, fear takes flight.

Where burdens weigh and troubles swell,
The soul discovers peace divine.
In whispered grace, we bid farewell,
To every storm, through love, we shine.

Nestled close, our spirits hear,
The sweet embrace of promises made.
In gentle hope, we cast our fear,
With every dawn, our faith displayed.

The refuge found within His care,
A sanctuary, warm and bright.
In every prayer, we lift the air,
With every tear, the path ignites.

Here in the silence, hearts unite,
In sacred trust, we step ahead.
From shadows thick, into the light,
We walk together, souls well-led.

## The Gift of Faithfulness

In whispers soft, the heart finds peace,
A promise held, it shall not cease.
Through trials faced, the spirit strong,
In faithfulness, we all belong.

In shadows deep, a light will glow,
A guiding star on paths we sow.
Through every storm, a steady hand,
In faith's embrace, together we'll stand.

With each new dawn, refresh our view,
In steadfast love, we start anew.
Each prayer a thread, we gently weave,
In faithfulness, the heart believes.

Through valleys low, and mountains high,
Our trust in Him will never die.
With open hearts, we share our plight,
In faithfulness, we find our light.

## Pathways of Loyalty

Steps marked with care, our journey calls,
With loyalty, our spirit sprawls.
In every choice, a bond we make,
Together strong, for love's own sake.

Through winding roads, with courage bold,
In loyalty, our hearts unfold.
With each small deed, we pave the way,
Through joy and pain, we choose to stay.

In storms that rise, our bond won't break,
With loyalty, our hearts awake.
A sacred trust that holds us near,
In every trial, we persevere.

With hands entwined, we brave the night,
In loyalty's warmth, we find our light.
Through laughter shared, and sorrows known,
In every step, we are not alone.

## **Fruits of Surrender**

In quiet hearts, the seeds are sown,
Through surrender, grace is grown.
A gentle clasp, we let it flow,
In yielding deep, we come to know.

With open hands, we give our all,
In surrender's dance, we rise and fall.
Through trials faced, we learn to trust,
In faithful love, we find what's just.

Each burden lifted, lightness swells,
In surrender's song, the spirit dwells.
With every hour, we seek the true,
Through love's embrace, we are made new.

In letting go, we find our way,
The fruits of love on display.
With hearts aligned, we seek to share,
The beauty found in faithful prayer.

## Embrace of Understanding

In silence shared, we find our voice,
In the embrace of understanding, we rejoice.
With open hearts, we seek to learn,
In every story, a trust we earn.

Through eyes that see, compassion flows,
In every moment, connection grows.
With kindness offered, barriers break,
In understanding, love we make.

In every face, the light we see,
A tapestry of humanity.
With gentle words, we build a bridge,
In understanding, we honor the pledge.

Through paths diverse, our hearts align,
In warmth of love, we find the divine.
With every hug, a bond we weave,
In embrace of understanding, we believe.

## **The Covenant of Hearts**

In silent whispers of the night,
Two souls unite in sacred light.
Through trials faced and joys they share,
A promise forged in fervent prayer.

With every breath, their spirits soar,
In love's embrace, they seek for more.
Through storm and calm, hand in hand,
Together, they will always stand.

In faith they nurture, hearts entwined,
Divine connection, ever kind.
With open hearts, they choose to trust,
In love's pure bond, they find their must.

Eternal vows, no fear can sever,
The light they hold, now and forever.
In every moment, grace will flow,
Their covenant in hearts will glow.

Through every trial, they shall sing,
To Him, their love, their offering.
In sacred union, they abide,
A testament of hearts, their guide.

## **Psalms of Surrender**

In stillness comes the heart's release,
In shadows deep, they find their peace.
With open arms, before the throne,
They lay their burdens, all alone.

The weight is lifted, light descends,
In gentle grace, their spirit mends.
With every tear, a prayer takes flight,
In surrender, they find the light.

The storm may roar, the winds may howl,
But in His arms, they softly bow.
For every trial, a lesson learned,
In love's embrace, their hearts have burned.

In gratitude, they find their song,
Through darkest days, they still stand strong.
With every note, their souls arise,
In fervent hymns that touch the skies.

To the Divine, their hearts they bring,
In quiet trust, they joyously sing.
For in surrender, they are free,
Forever tied in love's decree.

## The Tapestry of Trust

In woven threads of life so fine,
Each moment shared, a sacred sign.
With every stitch, a bond is sewn,
In faith's embrace, they are not alone.

Through trials faced, the colors blend,
A masterpiece that will not end.
In strength and hope, the fibers bind,
A tapestry of love designed.

With gentle hands, they weave their dreams,
A symphony of shared themes.
In laughter bright and sorrow's grace,
Together, they will find their place.

In beauty crafted, love reveals,
The truth that time and trust can heal.
With every thread, the stories weave,
In unity, they shall believe.

With faith as guide, they boldly step,
In every wound, a promise kept.
Through every trial, they will thrive,
In trust, they learn to truly live.

## Fables of Faithfulness

In ancient tales, their truth unfolds,
Of love so pure, of hearts so bold.
With every story, lessons shared,
In faithfulness, their spirits bared.

Through battles lost and victories won,
In kindred hearts, they find the sun.
With courage strong, they rise again,
In faith's embrace, there is no end.

They walk the path of trials and grace,
In every step, they find their place.
With hands upheld, they face the day,
In sacred bond, they choose to stay.

The flame of love, forever bright,
In every shadow, brings forth light.
With every promise, faithfulness grows,
In fables told, their love bestows.

In whispered prayers, they find their peace,
In every moment, love's increase.
Through all of time, their hearts remain,
In fables of faith, they break each chain.

## **Pilgrimage of Reliance**

In the shadows, I will tread,
With faith as my constant thread.
Each step a whispered prayer,
Guided by the Love I bear.

Mountains rise, yet I won't sway,
For in His arms, I find my way.
Through valleys deep and trials wide,
I walk with Him, my faithful guide.

The road winds on, yet I shall roam,
In every heart, I find my home.
Trust is the light that leads me on,
In the dawn, my spirit drawn.

Amongst the stones, His presence shines,
In every hymn, our spirit twines.
Together, we shall face the night,
Clinging to His guiding light.

A pilgrimage of heart and soul,
Each moment I surrender whole.
With every breath, I seek His grace,
In every trial, I see His face.

## The Gift of Assurance

In moments dark, a light appears,
Dissolving doubt, dispelling fears.
His whispers soft, a gentle balm,
In troubled seas, He keeps me calm.

The promise of dawn brings hope anew,
In every challenge, His love breaks through.
He gives me courage, unfailing trust,
In His embrace, I'm safe and just.

With open hands, I make my plea,
In silence, His peace comes over me.
Each breath a testament of grace,
In trials, I find His warm embrace.

His eyes, a mirror of my soul,
Reflecting love that makes me whole.
In every prayer, a bond is made,
Assurance blooms in faith conveyed.

Together, we shall share the load,
In every step of this sacred road.
The gift of assurance, ever near,
A steadfast promise, calm and clear.

## Fragrance of Devotion

In the quiet, my heart sings,
Of love that transcends earthly things.
With incense rising, spirits soar,
In acts of kindness, I implore.

Fragrance sweet, a blooming rose,
In every heart, His mercy flows.
Through daily service, I express,
The depth of my unhindered quest.

Compassion fuels my every stride,
In humble grace, I abide.
With open arms, I share the light,
In every soul, reflections bright.

The altar of my faith is clear,
In every action, He draws near.
A fragrance of devotion pure,
In love's embrace, I find the cure.

As petals fall, they paint the ground,
In loving deeds, my purpose found.
Through fragrant whispers, hope will rise,
In heartfelt moments, faith complies.

## **Atonement in Uncertainty**

In valleys low, I search my mind,
For peace and solace, intertwined.
Each fault, a step along the way,
In honest prayer, I learn to sway.

The weight of sin, a heavy chain,
Yet in His love, I'm free from pain.
Atonement sought through tears and fears,
In every heart, redemption nears.

With faith, I navigate the storm,
In every struggle, my soul transforms.
His mercy flows through shadows cast,
In fragile moments, my doubts surpassed.

The path unclear, yet hope's not lost,
In every burden, I bear the cost.
His light, a beacon shining bright,
Guiding me through the longest night.

Atonement found in love divine,
In shattered pieces, I see His sign.
Through uncertainty, my heart shall sing,
In every challenge, new life Spring.

## **Celestial Affection**

In the heavens high and bright,
Hearts unite in spiritual light,
Angels sing with voices clear,
Love divine is always near.

Beneath the stars, we find our way,
Guided by grace through night and day,
Hope ignites like a burning flame,
In our souls, we call His name.

Every tear, a lesson learned,
Through trials faced, our hearts have turned,
In celestial arms, we find peace,
Where all our doubts and sorrows cease.

Together we journey, hand in hand,
In faith's embrace, forever we stand,
Mountains moved by prayerful intent,
In celestial love, our lives are lent.

With hearts uplifted, we sing praise,
In worship's light, we spend our days,
Celestial affection, a gift so rare,
In every moment, He is there.

## Whispers of Faith

In the silence, whispers flow,
A gentle breeze, a soft glow,
Voices speak from the unseen,
Filling hearts with hopes serene.

Dreams bestowed on weary nights,
Guided by invisible lights,
Each step taken, a path of grace,
In faith's embrace, we find our place.

Through stormy seas and skies of gray,
Belief will always light the way,
With every prayer, our spirits rise,
In quiet moments, love never dies.

Beneath the weight of doubt and fear,
The whispers of faith we hold dear,
Drawing strength from a well within,
A sacred bond, where love begins.

In this journey, together we stand,
In the palms of a guiding hand,
Whispers of faith, life's sweet refrain,
In every heartbeat, love's domain.

## Bridges of Belief

Across the chasm, bridges rise,
Connecting hearts, uniting ties,
With faith as the foundation strong,
Together we will journey long.

Steps of courage, hand in hand,
Through valleys low and mountains grand,
In the light of trusting souls,
Our journey mends, and spirit tolls.

Faith in action, love displayed,
Through every choice, His light arrayed,
With open hearts, we mend the seams,
On bridges built of hope and dreams.

In unity, we share our plight,
Bound by love, shining bright,
For every heart that seeks to heal,
Bridges of belief, this sacred seal.

Together, we will stand the test,
Through trials faced, we're truly blessed,
In every laugh, in every tear,
Bridges of belief bring us near.

## Shadows of Doubt

In the corners where darkness creeps,
Shadows of doubt, their vigil keeps,
Yet a flicker of faith persists,
In the night, hope still exists.

Voices linger in whispered fears,
Echoes of past and fallen tears,
Yet light breaks through the cloudy veil,
With every prayer, we will prevail.

Though uncertainty may cloud our sight,
We fight our way towards the light,
In struggles faced, our spirits grow,
Through shadows, bright love will flow.

In trials we find our strength anew,
With hearts aligned, we'll see it through,
For in the depths of doubt's embrace,
We find redemption, saving grace.

So let us rise, our voices strong,
In faith's embrace, we all belong,
For even in the darkest night,
Shadows of doubt can't dim His light.

## **The Spirit of Connection**

In the silence, hearts entwine,
Whispers of love, pure and divine.
Threads of faith, woven tight,
A tapestry of joy and light.

Hands uplifted, souls align,
Binding us with a sacred sign.
Faithful footsteps on this road,
Together we bear each other's load.

Through every trial, love will grow,
In the garden where blessings flow.
Shared moments, hearts ablaze,
Together we walk in endless praise.

Unity in the vibrant dawn,
As dawn's first light spills on the lawn.
With every heartbeat, we find grace,
In the warmth of the divine embrace.

Oh, the spirit that we share,
Filling the world with loving care.
In connection, we discover peace,
A sacred bond that will not cease.

## **Sacred Echoes**

In the whispered prayers of the night,
Lies a truth, profound and bright.
Every heartbeat, a call to grace,
Echoes resound in this holy space.

Beneath the stars, hope takes flight,
Guided by faith, shining light.
Mirrored souls in a cosmic dance,
Each connection, a sacred chance.

Moments shared, a bond so rare,
Love's reflection, everywhere.
In the silence, we hear the song,
A melody where we all belong.

With every choice, a sacred vow,
In the present, we honor the now.
Through trials faced and joys we find,
The echoes of love, forever entwined.

In the tapestry of night sky's hue,
Weaving stories, forever true.
In echoes of kindness, we rise,
Finding solace in each other's eyes.

## The Promise of Tomorrow

In the dawn, a vision clear,
Hope arises, casting out fear.
With each breath, new dreams ignite,
A promise shines, restoring the light.

Seeds of faith in the soil we sow,
Watered by love, destined to grow.
Through shadows that may obscure the view,
The promise glows in every hue.

In the stillness, answers unfold,
A journey of stories yet untold.
Together we walk through the unknown,
Trusting the goodness that we've grown.

With open hearts, we dare to explore,
Each step forward, we seek for more.
A boundless future, hand in hand,
In shared visions, we take our stand.

In the light of a brand new day,
Woven together in love's array.
The promise sings, forever bright,
Guiding us toward eternal light.

## The Chalice of Commitment

In gatherings where spirits blend,
We raise the chalice, love our friend.
A sacred drink from hearts that care,
With each sip, we take the dare.

Vows exchanged in humble grace,
A holy bond time can't erase.
Through trials faced, we stand as one,
In the warmth of love's bright sun.

Through darkness and into light,
Together we rise, hearts taking flight.
In every promise, a spark glows,
The chalice flows as kindness shows.

With open minds, we seek to share,
The burdens lifted in heartfelt prayer.
In the commitment, a life unfolds,
A story written in love untold.

In the gathering, unity sings,
The chalice brimming with hopeful things.
Together we journey, never apart,
In the chalice of commitment, we start.

# Echoes of the Heart

In silence He whispers, soft and near,
Guiding the lost, calming the fear.
With faith as a lantern, bright and clear,
We walk with Him, our way sincere.

In shadows we find His gentle call,
A promise of love, to cradle all.
With each heartfelt prayer, we rise and fall,
His grace lifts us, we hear His thrall.

Through trials and storms, He leads the way,
In the darkened hours, we choose to stay.
With every heartbeat, we learn to pray,
Trusting in Him, come what may.

In echoes profound, our spirits sing,
A hymn of surrender, to Him we cling.
In the melody of life, we find spring,
Each note a reflection of what He brings.

In unity we stand, hearts intertwined,
With love and compassion, forever aligned.
His truth is the balm, our souls refined,
In the echoes of the heart, Heaven defined.

## The Pathway of Certainty

Upon this path, unwavering tread,
Where doubts dissolve, and fears are shed.
With every step, His light we spread,
Guiding the weary, their hearts are fed.

In every season, His promise stands,
With open arms, He understands.
Through trials fierce, and shifting sands,
His love remains, forever lands.

With voices lifted, we sing of trust,
In Him we find a hope robust.
Guiding our souls with love so just,
Upon this journey, in Him we must.

As shadows fade, His glory shines,
Each moment a gift in sacred signs.
In Him we find our lives align,
The pathway of certainty, divine.

With every sunrise, new mercies greet,
His faithfulness, our hearts' heartbeat.
In the tapestry of life, we meet,
On the pathway of certainty, complete.

## Parables of the Soul

In stories profound, His wisdom glows,
With every parable, the heart knows.
Seeds of truth in the silence grows,
A tapestry woven, where love flows.

Amidst the struggles, His voice is clear,
Each lesson shared, we hold so dear.
In every trial, His grace appears,
Transforming our pain into holy cheers.

Through humble fields, His whispers guide,
In compassion's embrace, we abide.
A fable of mercy, drawn aside,
In the parables, our souls confide.

With hearts open wide, we seek to learn,
Through faith and trust, our spirits burn.
In the garden of hope, we yearn,
For every parable, a heart's return.

In the shadows bright, His stories dance,
Each moment a treasure, a sacred chance.
Through the parables, our souls enhance,
In love's embrace, we find romance.

## **The Sanctuary of Confidence**

In this sanctuary, hearts unite,
A haven of faith, where souls take flight.
With trust in the unseen, fears take flight,
In His presence, we shine so bright.

Within these walls, love flows like streams,
A refuge of hope, fulfilling dreams.
With prayers ascending, our spirit beams,
In God's embrace, we find our themes.

Through trials faced, He guides the way,
In every tear, He wipes away.
With courage reborn, we rise each day,
In the sanctuary, come what may.

With hearts of gold, we boldly stand,
In the light of His love, forever planned.
Hand in hand together, we'll expand,
In the sanctuary, hope is our brand.

In every heartbeat, His peace we claim,
With confidence rooted, we praise His name.
Together as one, igniting the flame,
In the sanctuary, our hearts proclaim.

# The Altar of Reliability

In the quiet shadows where faith resides,
We gather our hopes, our hearts open wide.
Each promise whispered, a sacred decree,
Sustained through the trials, unwaveringly free.

Trust is the base, a foundation so true,
In the warmth of connection, old and anew.
Together we stand, in prayer's gentle fold,
We share our stories, both timid and bold.

On the altar of trust, we place all we own,
With love as our currency, we're never alone.
In moments of doubt, we will strengthen each other,
For in this divine bond, we all are a mother.

With every heartbeat, we find our way back,
To the sacred embrace, a welcoming track.
In the tapestry woven from threads of the past,
We hold on together, united and steadfast.

Let us cherish the moments, both joyous and dire,
For the altar of reliability fuels our fire.
In unity's name, we blossom and thrive,
In the arms of our faith, together we live.

## **Waters of Serenity**

By the gentle stream where the soft willows sway,
We listen to whispers that guide us each day.
With hearts like the water, so pure and so clear,
We seek the redemption that love can endear.

As ripples unfold in the dance of the breeze,
We feel every blessing bring comfort and ease.
The waters invite us to cast away strife,
In their tranquil embrace, we find joyful life.

Beneath azure skies, we gather and pray,
In the flow of divinity, we trust and obey.
With faith like a torrent, we cleanse troubled souls,
Washing away fears, making broken hearts whole.

Let the waters of faith wash over us all,
In the stillness divine, we heed the soft call.
For in unity's flow, we are strengthened and free,
In the waters of serenity, our spirits agree.

So come to the river, let your burdens release,
In the currents of grace, we shall find our peace.
Together we stand, as we drink from this spring,
In the warmth of our faith, forever we sing.

## Beneath the Willow's Watch

Underneath the willow, we find sacred rest,
Its branches embrace us, a nurturing nest.
In the stillness we gather, our prayers gently rise,
With gratitude offered in soft, whispered sighs.

A refuge of solace, beneath leafy shade,
We share our confessions, unafraid and unchafed.
In the dance of the leaves, a rhythm we know,
Each heartbeat connected, like rivers we flow.

In the heart of the moment, we cherish the grace,
Of fellowship woven in this holy space.
With laughter and tears, we find joy and release,
Amidst nature's embrace, our spirits increase.

As the sun slowly sinks, we hold hands in peace,
A tapestry forming, our sorrows will cease.
For beneath the old willow, love binds us as one,
In the warmth of connection, new journeys begun.

So come gather near, let your burdens unwind,
Underneath the willow, let faith be our guide.
In the hush of the twilight, our hearts intertwined,
We tread the path forward, with God we will find.

## Tapestry of Fellowship

Threads of compassion, intricately spun,
A tapestry finished, yet always begun.
With colors of kindness, we weave our design,
In the fabric of grace, our hearts intertwine.

In moments of silence, our spirits take flight,
As the tapestry shifts with the day into night.
With every new heartbeat, a pattern we see,
Fellowship blossoming, from you unto me.

Let love be the needle that mends every seam,
Together we flourish, united we dream.
In the warmth of connection, our souls are consoled,
As we dance in the fabric, together and bold.

Each story a stitch, with wisdom to share,
In the tapestry's beauty, we lift up our prayer.
To cherish each moment, each thread that we see,
In this blessed assembly, we flourish and free.

So gather, dear friends, as we hold this space close,
In the tapestry woven, we flourish the most.
For in each other's presence, our spirits ascend,
In the tapestry of fellowship, love has no end.

## **The Gospel of Hope**

In shadows deep, a light shall bloom,
With faithful hearts, dispelling gloom.
Each whispered prayer, a soothing balm,
In trials faced, find peace and calm.

The dawn will break, the night will flee,
In every soul, there's victory.
A promise made, forever true,
With open arms, His love renews.

Through valleys low, and mountains high,
In every tear, the heart shall cry.
Yet hope shall rise on wings of grace,
To find the strength in His embrace.

With faith as shield, we face the storm,
In darkest days, His light is warm.
In every trial, we will stand,
United strong, hand in hand.

The Gospel speaks, of love's great reign,
In every heart, He breaks the chain.
For hope is found, in every song,
With faith in Him, we shall be strong.

## **Psalm of the Unseen**

In silence deep, the spirit sighs,
Beyond the veil, the truth replies.
With willing hearts, we seek the light,
In shadows cast, He ends the night.

The world may fade, yet faith stands tall,
In every rise, in every fall.
For what is seen will soon depart,
Yet unseen grace fills every heart.

Through trials fierce, our spirits soar,
In whispered winds, we hear His roar.
The unseen hands that guide our way,
For love abounds in every day.

With every tear, a lesson learned,
In darkest paths, the heart's still yearned.
For faith's the bridge, the light we seek,
In every soul, He finds the weak.

In quietude, we find our peace,
In every prayer, His love won't cease.
With eyes of faith, we see the way,
For in His arms, we're not astray.

# The Embrace of Reliability

In every storm, He stands so near,
With outstretched arms, we have no fear.
For in His hands, our hearts reside,
In every step, He is our guide.

Through trials vast, and moments brief,
He offers hope, a sweet relief.
With every sigh, He hears our call,
In every rise, He lifts us all.

When paths grow dark, and doubts arise,
In faith we stand, beneath the skies.
For what remains, when all is lost,
Is love unyielding, no matter the cost.

His promises, a steadfast light,
In every wrong, He makes it right.
In every heart that feels alone,
The embrace of love, we call our own.

With every leap, we trust the plan,
For in His gaze, a loving span.
In every breath, reliability,
Our anchor firm, our certainty.

## **Treasures of the Spirit**

In quiet corners of the soul,
Lie treasures deep, to make us whole.
With every breath, a gift is found,
In whispered prayers, our hearts resound.

Each act of love, a shining prize,
In kindness spread, our spirits rise.
For wealth unseen, within us gleams,
As faith ignites our hopeful dreams.

Through trials faced, and paths unknown,
In every seed of love we've sown.
The spirit dances, free and bold,
In every tale of grace retold.

With eyes anew, we seek the truth,
In every age, in every youth.
The treasures lie in hearts sincere,
In steadfast faith, we draw Him near.

Each moment lived, a chance to shine,
In hope we trust, for love divine.
For treasures grow, when spirits sing,
In every heart, new life takes wing.

## **Whispers of Faith**

In silence, soft whispers rise,
Hearts awakened to the skies.
Faithful shadows in the night,
Guiding souls towards the light.

Trust the path that love has paved,
In the storms, find hearts that braved.
Together, we'll tread on stone,
In His arms, we are not alone.

Each prayer a sparkling star,
Reminding us just who we are.
In the dark, His grace will glow,
Through every trial, love will flow.

With every breath, we seek the truth,
Embrace the words of eternal youth.
In kindness, our spirits soar,
In whispers of faith, we explore.

When doubt creeps, let love take hold,
In the stories of old, we're told.
With open hearts, we'll rise above,
Wrapped in the warmth of divine love.

## **Threads of Belief**

Woven tightly, threads of grace,
In every heart, a sacred place.
We stitch our dreams with love's own hands,
In unity, our spirit stands.

Each strand a story, richly sewn,
In faith's embrace, we're never lone.
Together, hand in hand we walk,
In whispers soft, our spirits talk.

Through trials faced and mountains high,
With threads of belief, we touch the sky.
Unraveling fears, we boldly tread,
In the light of love, no tears to shed.

Let every choice be steeped in love,
Guided by the stars above.
With patience, we shall mend each tear,
In whispered prayers, we find our care.

For in the tapestry we create,
Each thread connects, we cultivate.
In joy and sorrow, together we weave,
In the fabric of belief, we believe.

## Shadows of Devotion

In quiet moments when we pray,
Devotion wraps us, come what may.
In shadows cast by love's embrace,
We find our strength, a sacred space.

With each heartbeat, our vows renew,
In silence, whispers guide us true.
Through valleys low and mountains steep,
In shadows of devotion, we keep.

Touch the earth with gentle hands,
In every heart, His message stands.
In every challenge, courage grows,
With steadfast faith, the spirit glows.

Through trials faced, our hope will shine,
In shadows deep, the stars align.
Together bound by love's decree,
In shadows of devotion, we see.

Let our light break through despair,
A testament of love laid bare.
In unity, we rise above,
Together, we share His endless love.

## **The Bridge of Assurance**

Across the chasm, faith will bridge,
In every heart, a love's big whidge.
With open arms, we take each stride,
In the river of grace, love won't hide.

Through storms that rage and winds that sigh,
Together we'll soar, as birds we fly.
This bridge of assurance, strong and wide,
With every heartbeat, joy our guide.

Forging paths through shadows long,
In harmony, we sing the song.
In every step, in every tear,
This bridge of assurance draws us near.

With faith as our lantern, leading the way,
We find our strength, come what may.
In the embrace of His watchful care,
The bridge of assurance, we're never bare.

Together we'll cross, hand in hand,
In love's embrace, we make our stand.
Faithful hearts, forever sure,
With every stride, our love will endure.

## The Oasis of Belief

In the quiet desert night,
The stars whisper hope so bright.
Mirage fades, truth appears,
Faith's oasis calms our fears.

Water flows from sacred springs,
Life and joy, the spirit sings.
In this place, the heart finds rest,
In belief, we are truly blessed.

Seek the path where love abides,
In every tear, His mercy hides.
Miracles are born from prayer,
In the oasis, burdens share.

With open hands, we receive grace,
In each moment, we find His face.
Together in this sacred space,
We walk, we trust, we embrace.

Blissful peace, like water clear,
Strengthens resolve, calms every fear.
With faith, we rise, with hearts set free,
In the depths of belief, we see.

## **Veils of Faith**

Veils of faith softly descend,
Trusting the journey without end.
Every thread, a promise spun,
In His light, we are all one.

Shadows linger, doubts may rise,
Yet in Him, our spirit flies.
Through the veils, we glimpse the truth,
A loving heart, eternal youth.

Faith unfurls like petals bright,
Guiding souls through darkest night.
With every heartbeat, we proclaim,
In His name, we find no shame.

Wrapped in grace, we walk the line,
Each step a dance, divine design.
Veils of faith, our spirits blend,
In mercy's arms, we find our friend.

Lifted high, our voices soar,
In unison, we seek for more.
Through trials faced, we hold the light,
Veils of faith guide us to right.

## The Flame of Assurance

From tender sparks, a flame ignites,
A beacon in the darkest nights.
In every heart, a warmth resides,
With God beside, our faith abides.

Assurance burns, a steadfast guide,
In troubles faced, He will provide.
With every flicker, doubts depart,
His light ignites our weary heart.

In trials' storm, it flickers bright,
A steady glow, our path alight.
Embracing love, we rise above,
In the flame, we find His love.

Through winds that howl and tempests roar,
The flame endures forevermore.
With faith ablaze, we hold it dear,
His flame of assurance casts out fear.

Together, we fan this holy light,
Igniting hope, dispelling night.
Faith's flame within, forever stays,
Guiding us in wondrous ways.

## The Garden of Loyalty

In the garden where hearts align,
Roots of loyalty intertwine.
Thorns of doubt may try to grow,
Yet in faith, Love's river flows.

Each blossom sings a sacred song,
In unity, we all belong.
Through trials faced, we cultivate,
In loyalty, we navigate.

Nurtured by the light above,
In every bloom, we feel His love.
Together, we tend the fields of grace,
In this garden, we find our place.

Seasons change, but we remain,
With roots of faith, we bear the strain.
In loyalty's embrace, we stand tall,
Together, bound, we never fall.

Harvests yield from hearts sincere,
In the garden, we persevere.
With grateful hearts, we sow the seeds,
In the garden of loyalty, we find our needs.

# Foundations of Truth

In the silence of the dawn, we seek,
Wisdom whispers soft and meek.
Upon the stone, our faith does stand,
Anchored deep in a sacred land.

In shadows cast by doubt's cruel hand,
Hope springs forth, a golden strand.
With hearts aligned to heaven's call,
We rise in grace, united all.

Each gentle breeze, a prayer sent high,
To the One who hears our cries.
In every tear, a lesson learned,
The flame of love forever burns.

Through trials faced and storms that rage,
We turn the page, a new stage.
In unity, we find our way,
Together strong, come what may.

The truth will stand, unshaken, strong,
An eternal light where we belong.
Foundations laid, we walk in grace,
In the arms of the divine embrace.

## The Aria of Belief

In the stillness, melodies arise,
Whispers of faith in the skies.
Voices join, a sacred choir,
Singing praises to the Holy Fire.

Each note a journey, heart to heart,
In every rhythm, we take part.
With open souls, we seek to find,
Harmony in the divine mind.

Through valleys low and mountains high,
Our spirits rise, we dare to fly.
In every struggle, courage grows,
Through darkest nights, the light still glows.

The aria echoes, pure and true,
A tapestry woven anew.
In this song, we find our peace,
An everlasting, sweet release.

Let every heart join hand in hand,
Together strong, together stand.
In the symphony of grace, we sing,
Life's eternal, sacred ring.

# Canopy of Reliability

Beneath the boughs of love we find,
A shelter for the weary mind.
In trials faced, we look above,
A canopy of steadfast love.

Through storms that shake and winds that howl,
We stand as one, we will not bow.
With trust as our unyielding guide,
In faith, our fears will swiftly slide.

Each leaf a promise, green and bright,
In darkest times, we seek the light.
The roots run deep, entwined as one,
In the embrace of the Holy Son.

Together we weave a tapestry,
Of hope and love, our legacy.
Under this shelter, we find rest,
In truth's embrace, we are blessed.

The canopy stands through every trial,
A testament of faith, our eternal smile.
Through valleys low and skies so wide,
We walk with Him, forever side by side.

# Emblems of Fidelity

In the heart, loyalty abides,
A compass true, where love resides.
With steadfastness, we bear the load,
Emblems of fidelity on the road.

In every promise, words that bind,
A sacred bond, in love aligned.
In trials faced and joys we share,
United hearts, in fervent prayer.

Through seasons changing, trust holds strong,
In unity, we all belong.
With hands held high, we shall aspire,
To lift each other, never tire.

Each commitment, a cherished vow,
In every moment, here and now.
In faithfulness, our spirits soar,
Together we seek, forevermore.

The emblems shine, both bright and grand,
A testament to love's pure hand.
Through every trial, we shall abide,
In the light of truth, forever guide.

# Portals of Faith's Glisten

In the quiet glow, a promise lies,
Hearts uplifted, we gaze to the skies.
Through every shadow, His light we seek,
With whispers of hope that strengthen the meek.

In the stillness, there's peace to find,
As we open our hearts and look to the Kind.
Paths of grace lead us, though frail we stand,
Each step a blessing, each touch a hand.

Through trials faced, our spirits soar,
In the warmth of faith, we yearn for more.
The portals wide, let love cascade,
In sacred spaces, our fears allayed.

A journey shared at dawn's first light,
With every heartbeat, our souls ignite.
The trail of trust, in unity we tread,
With prayers like lanterns, our spirits fed.

So let us wander where the spirit calls,
In heavenly verses, where devotion falls.
For in the glisten, eternity waits,
Beyond the portals, love celebrates.

## **Gossamer Threads of Assurance**

In fragile whispers, trust is spun,
Gossamer threads, beneath the sun.
A tapestry woven with tender care,
Each moment of doubt, a prayer laid bare.

Through the tempest, hope does shine,
An anchor firm, in love divine.
We gather strength from the heart's embrace,
In the arms of faith, we find our place.

Life's journey is blessed with gentle grace,
We carry the light, a sacred space.
Together we rise, through storms we sail,
On gossamer threads, our spirits prevail.

Each promise echoes in the still of night,
A chorus of souls, united in light.
With certainty woven in every strand,
In faith's embrace, together we stand.

Here in the silence, we find our song,
With every heartbeat, we know we belong.
Through gossamer threads, our fears take flight,
In the glow of assurance, we shine so bright.

## The Steeple of Belief

High above, the steeple stands tall,
A sacred tower, inviting us all.
With arms open wide, it calls us near,
To gather in love, to conquer our fear.

Around its base, the faithful convene,
In a dance of joy, where hope is seen.
Each voice a melody, a song of grace,
In the steeple's shadow, we find our place.

As shadows lengthen, and dusk draws near,
We light our candles, dispelling fear.
The warmth of faith, it lightly beams,
In the heart of the steeple, we chase our dreams.

Through trials and storms, we lift our gaze,
Towards the heavens, in our fervent praise.
The steeple glows in the twilight hue,
A beacon of truth that guides us through.

So let us gather, beneath its arms wide,
In the steeple of belief, where love abides.
A sanctuary built on enduring trust,
Together we flourish; together we must.

## The Lantern in the Abyss

In the depths of despair, a lantern shines,
Its light a guide through darkened times.
As shadows dance, we find our way,
With faith as our compass, night turns to day.

The abyss may beckon with whispers of doubt,
Yet the lantern's glow, we cannot live without.
Each flickering flame, a promise kept,
In the silence of night, our souls are adept.

With every heartbeat, the light will grow,
Illuminating truths we yearn to know.
Through the darkest valleys, we'll boldly tread,
With the lantern aglow, no need to dread.

Together we rise, hearts intertwined,
In the warmth of belief, our spirits aligned.
So let us journey where shadows might play,
With the lantern in hand, we'll find our way.

In faith we gather, our burdens released,
With the lantern of hope, our fears decreased.
The abyss may whisper, but won't lead astray,
For within us burns a light that won't sway.

## Wings of Assurance

In the shadow of the sacred light,
Angels gather, soaring in flight.
With faith as our strength, we rise above,
On wings of assurance, wrapped in love.

Through trials and storms, we hold His hand,
In each whispered prayer, we firmly stand.
With grace bestowed, our hearts unite,
Guided forever by the holy might.

In valleys deep, where shadows play,
His promise shines, illuminating the way.
With every heartbeat, our spirits sing,
Eternal blessings on love's soft wing.

Among the weary, we find our peace,
In fervent belief, our doubts release.
For every tear, a joy shall bloom,
In the light of His love, dispelling gloom.

So let faith blossom within our soul,
With wings of assurance, we become whole.
In the sanctuary of grace divine,
Together we flourish, forever entwined.

## **The Garden of Fidelity**

In the garden where love is sown,
Beneath the sky, where blessings have grown.
With each tender root, our bond strengthens wide,
In the grace of fidelity, we abide.

The flowers of trust, in colors so bright,
Bloom in the warmth of His guiding light.
Every promise made, a seed we plant,
With hearts intertwined, and hope ever scant.

Through seasons of change, we shall endure,
With love as our shield, steadfast and pure.
In the whispers of faith, we find our way,
In the garden of fidelity, we choose to stay.

The fruits of our labor, both sweet and bold,
In unity bound, our story unfolds.
With each fragrant petal, we honor the past,
For in love's rich soil, our roots hold fast.

So cherish the moments, let kindness flow,
In this sacred garden, let compassion grow.
With every heartbeat, may love be our creed,
Finding solace in giving, fulfilling each need.

## **The Sanctuary of Hope**

In the quiet depths of our sacred space,
Hope takes refuge, a warm embrace.
In whispered prayers, hearts find their tune,
In the sanctuary of hope, love's bright boon.

With every dawn, a new chance bestowed,
To rise with the light, as faith is flowed.
In shadows that linger, we lift our gaze,
With dreams intertwined, through life's winding maze.

Each promise of peace, ignites the soul,
In the warmth of His presence, we become whole.
Through trials and tears, we forge our path,
In the sanctuary of hope, we embrace His wrath.

With every heartbeat, our spirits soar,
In the embrace of love, we seek to explore.
For in every struggle, a lesson laid bare,
In hope's vibrant glow, our hearts we share.

So let us gather, hand in hand we stand,
In the sanctuary of hope, forever planned.
With every breath, our souls ignite,
In love's gentle whispers, we find our light.

## **Communion of Souls**

In the sacred union where spirits align,
A communion of souls, forever divine.
With hearts intertwined, in the cosmic dance,
We share in the love, in fate's gentle chance.

Through laughter and tears, we travel this road,
In the light of His glory, we lighten our load.
With every heartbeat, a rhythm we find,
In the sacred embrace, our souls are combined.

The echoes of wisdom whisper so clear,
In the presence of love, we cast out our fear.
With every prayer spoken, a bond is reinforced,
In the communion of souls, our spirits, endorsed.

In moments of stillness, together we tread,
In the heart of our journey, our spirits are fed.
For in love's true essence, we find our grace,
In the communion of souls, we claim our place.

So let us gather, in the warmth of the light,
In this holy union, forever in flight.
With every step forward, our spirits unfold,
In unity grounded, our stories are told.